FLORIDA TRAVEL GUIDE

Explore Hidden Wonders, Iconic Destinations, and Unforgettable Adventures in the Sunshine State

LYLAH VEGA

Copyright© 2025 Lylah Vega. All Rights Reserved.

Without the publisher's prior written permission, no part of this publication may be reproduced, distributed, or transmitted in any form or by any means, including photocopying, recording, or other electronic or mechanical methods, with the exception of brief quotations in critical reviews and certain other non-commercial uses permitted by copyright law.

TABLE OF CONTENTS

MAP 7
INTRODUCTION 8
   Why Florida in 2025? 8
   Best Times to Visit Florida 9
   Florida at a Glance: Quick Facts and Highlights 11
PLANNING YOUR TRIP 12
   Essential Travel Tips for Florida 12
   Packing Checklist 13
   Transportation Options 15
FLORIDA'S BEACHES AND COASTAL ESCAPES 18
   The Gulf Coast 18
   The Atlantic Coast 20
ORLANDO AND THEME PARK MAGIC 22
   Walt Disney World 22
   Universal Orlando: Thrills and Innovations 25
   Lesser-Known Theme Parks and Attractions 27
WILDLIFE AND NATURE ADVENTURES 29
   The Everglades: A UNESCO World Heritage Site 29
   State Parks and Scenic Trails 30
   Florida's Unique Wildlife 32
CITY HIGHLIGHTS 34
   Miami 34
   Tampa Bay 35
   Jacksonville 37
   Tallahassee 38
   St. Petersburg and Clearwater 40
   Fort Lauderdale 41
THE FLORIDA KEYS: ISLAND ESCAPES AND ENDLESS ADVENTURE 42
   Introduction to the Florida Keys 42

    Key Islands and Highlights 43
    Key West.. 47
    Duval Street.. 49
    Southernmost Point... 50
    Outdoor Activities.. 51

CULTURAL AND HISTORICAL SITES.. 53

St. Augustine: The Nation's Oldest City............................53
    Cuban Heritage in Key West.. 54
    Native American History and Archaeological Sites............... 55

OUTDOOR ADVENTURES AND SPORTS....................................56
    Snorkeling and Diving Hotspots 56
    Golfing in the Sunshine... 57
    State Kayaking, Paddleboarding, and Fishing.....................58

FOOD AND DRINK IN FLORIDA 59
    Iconic Dishes.. 59

Florida's Culinary Scene...60
    Local Drinks..61
    Restaurants in Florida... 62

SHOPPING AND SOUVENIRS... 64
    Best Shopping Destinations... 64
    Unique Florida Souvenirs 66
    Outlet Shopping Tips 67

ACCOMMODATIONS IN FLORIDA...69
    Luxury Resorts and Hotels 69
    Budget-Friendly Options 70
    Unique Stays.. 72

SEASONAL EVENTS AND FESTIVALS...74
    Music Festivals: From EDM to Jazz 74
    Art Shows, Parades, and Cultural Events............................75
    Sports Events and Tournaments.. 76

HIDDEN GEMS IN FLORIDA... 78
    Off-the-Beaten-Path Destinations.. 78

Underrated Small Towns..80
SCENIC DRIVES AND ROAD TRIP ROUTES.......................81
The Overseas Highway: A Drive to Remember......................81
A1A Coastal Byway..82
Historic Tamiami Trail..83
FLORIDA FOR FAMILIES..85
Kid-Friendly Attractions..85
Tips for Traveling with Kids..86
KID-FRIENDLY ACCOMMODATIONS.....................................87
Best Family Beaches...89
PRACTICAL INFORMATION...91
Travel Safety in Florida..91
Weather and Hurricane Season Tips.......................................92
Important Contacts and Resources..93
CONCLUSION...96
Final Tips for a Memorable Trip...96
Florida Beyond 2025: What's Next..97

MAP

INTRODUCTION

Why Florida in 2025?

Florida, the Sunshine State, remains one of the most sought-after travel destinations in the world. In 2025, Florida offers an exceptional blend of natural beauty, cultural diversity, and year-round outdoor activities that make it a top choice for travelers. Whether looking for pristine beaches, thrilling theme parks, or rich history, Florida has something for everyone.

The state's iconic coastline stretches for over 1,300 miles, providing endless opportunities for beach lovers, with famous spots like Miami Beach, Clearwater, and the Florida Keys. Beyond the beaches, Florida's national parks, including Everglades National Park and Dry Tortugas, offer rare glimpses into unique ecosystems teeming with wildlife.

Florida is also home to world-class attractions, particularly the theme parks in Orlando, where Disney, Universal, and SeaWorld provide unforgettable experiences. Meanwhile, cities like Miami, with its vibrant arts scene and nightlife, and St. Augustine, the oldest city in the U.S., offer rich cultural experiences.

In 2025, Florida's travel infrastructure will continue to improve, with enhanced transportation networks and eco-friendly initiatives promoting sustainability. From adventure enthusiasts to culture seekers, Florida's diverse offerings ensure that visitors will have an unforgettable experience, making it a perfect destination for any traveler in 2025.

Best Times to Visit Florida

Florida offers a year-round appeal, but the best time to visit depends on your preferences for weather, activities, and crowds.

Winter (December - February):
Winter is arguably the most popular time to visit Florida, especially for those seeking to escape colder climates. The weather is mild and comfortable, with daytime temperatures ranging from 65°F to 75°F (18°C to 24°C). This season is perfect for outdoor activities, beach

vacations, and theme parks. However, it's also peak tourist season, so expect larger crowds, especially around holidays like Christmas and New Year's.

Spring (March-May):
Spring offers a sweet spot for visitors. The weather is warm but not too hot, with temperatures ranging from 70°F to 85°F (21°C to 29°C). This is the ideal time for outdoor exploration, including hiking, biking, and sightseeing. Spring break, particularly in March, can bring larger crowds, especially to cities like Miami and Orlando. Still, overall, the season offers a mix of great weather and fewer tourists than winter.

Summer (June - August):
Summer is the hottest time in Florida, with temperatures soaring above 90°F (32°C). While it's great for beachgoers and water sports enthusiasts, the heat can be intense, and humidity levels are high. Expect afternoon thunderstorms, particularly in the central and southern regions.

Fall (September - November):
Fall is the least crowded time to visit Florida. The weather starts to cool slightly, with temperatures averaging 75°F to 85°F (24°C to 29°C). Hurricane season peaks in September and October, so it's important to monitor the weather, but the lack of crowds makes it an attractive option for a quieter trip.

Florida at a Glance: Quick Facts and Highlights

Florida, sometimes referred to as the "Sunshine State," is situated in the southeastern region of the United States. It is the 22nd largest state by land area and the third most populous, with over 21 million residents. The state is bordered by the Atlantic Ocean to the east, the Gulf of Mexico to the west, and Alabama and Georgia to the north. Known for its warm, tropical climate, Florida is a year-round destination for travelers seeking sunshine and outdoor activities.

Key Highlights:

- **Beaches:** Florida boasts over 1,300 miles of coastline, offering pristine beaches like those in the Florida Keys, South Beach in Miami, and Clearwater Beach.

- **Theme Parks:** Home to world-renowned attractions, including Walt Disney World, Universal Studios, and SeaWorld in Orlando.

- **Everglades National Park:** A UNESCO World Heritage site and the largest tropical wilderness in the U.S., famous for its diverse wildlife and unique ecosystem.

- **Cultural Cities**: Miami is renowned for its vibrant arts scene and Cuban influence, while St. Augustine, the oldest city in the U.S., offers a rich history and colonial architecture.

- **Outdoor Adventures:** From kayaking through mangroves to exploring the Appalachian Trail's southern terminus, Florida offers diverse landscapes for adventure enthusiasts.

PLANNING YOUR TRIP

Essential Travel Tips for Florida

Navigating Florida can be exciting and overwhelming, so here are key tips to ensure a smooth trip.

1. Best Time to Visit:
Florida enjoys warm weather year-round, but the peak tourist season runs from December to April. For lower crowds and cheaper rates, consider visiting in the off-season (May to November), keeping in mind that summer can be hot and rainy.

2. Packing Essentials:
Light clothing is essential due to Florida's warm climate. Don't forget sunscreen, comfortable shoes for walking, swimwear, and a rain jacket for unpredictable showers. Also, bring bug repellent for areas near water, especially during summer.

3. Transportation:
Renting a car is recommended for getting around the state, especially outside major cities. While public transportation exists in larger areas, having a car offers flexibility. Be prepared for traffic, particularly in cities like Miami, Orlando, and Tampa.

4. Weather Considerations:
Florida's weather can be unpredictable. Always check the forecast before your trip, especially during hurricane season (June to November). Stay informed on weather advisories and plan accordingly.

5. Safety Tips:
Stay hydrated in the heat, use sunscreen, and be cautious in unfamiliar areas. Also, keep a copy of your travel documents, in case of emergencies.

Packing Checklist

Packing for a Florida adventure requires thoughtful preparation, ensuring you're ready for its diverse activities, climates, and unique experiences. Here's a comprehensive checklist to guide your packing:

Clothing:
- Light, breathable fabrics (cotton, linen) for hot days.

- Swimwear for beach trips or resort pools.
- Comfortable walking shoes for theme parks, city tours, or nature hikes.
- For chilly evenings, particularly in coastal regions, wear a light jacket or jumper.
- Rain gear, like an umbrella or poncho, for Florida's frequent afternoon showers.
- Sunglasses and hats for sun protection.

Toiletries:
- Sunscreen (reef-safe) to protect against Florida's strong sun.
- Bug repellent, especially for nature activities or swamp tours.
- Personal hygiene items (toothbrush, shampoo, deodorant).

Tech:
- Phone and charger.
- Portable power bank for long days out.
- Camera to capture Florida's scenic beauty.

Documents:
- ID, tickets, and hotel reservation confirmations.
- Credit cards/cash.

Transportation Options

Getting There

By Air:
Florida boasts several major airports, making air travel one of the most convenient ways to arrive.

- **Miami International Airport (MIA):** A bustling hub for international and domestic flights.
- **Orlando International Airport (MCO):** Perfect for accessing theme parks and central Florida.
- **Tampa International Airport (TPA):** Serving the Gulf Coast with efficiency and charm.
- **Fort Lauderdale-Hollywood International Airport (FLL):** Ideal for travelers heading to South Florida.

By Car:
Driving into Florida offers stunning views and flexibility:

- **Interstate 95 (I-95):** Runs along the East Coast, connecting Florida to cities like New York, Washington, and Savannah.
- **Interstate 75 (I-75):** A popular route for travelers from the Midwest and Southern states.
- **Overseas Highway (U.S. Route 1):** A scenic marvel that connects mainland Florida to the Keys, offering breathtaking ocean views.

By Train:
- **Silver Star and Silver Meteor Routes:** These lines serve Florida's major cities, including Jacksonville, Tampa, Orlando, and Miami, offering a scenic ride through the East Coast.

By Sea:
Florida's ports welcome cruise travelers in style:

- **PortMiami:** Known as the "Cruise Capital of the World."

- **Port Everglades (Fort Lauderdale):** A hub for Caribbean cruises.

- **Other Ports:** Tampa, Jacksonville, and Port Canaveral also offer cruise arrivals.

Getting Around

Florida's vast landscape offers a variety of transportation options, making it easy for visitors to explore the state's many attractions. Whether you're traveling between cities, heading to the beach, or navigating theme parks, here's a guide to getting around Florida:

- **By Car:** One of the most common ways to get around Florida is by renting a car. With major highways like I-95, I-75, and the Florida Turnpike connecting key destinations, driving offers flexibility and convenience. Rental cars are available at airports and throughout cities, but be prepared for traffic, especially around tourist hubs like Miami, Orlando, and Tampa.

- **Public Transit:** Florida's public transportation systems vary by city. Miami boasts the Metrorail, Metromover, and buses, while

Orlando has buses and the SunRail commuter service. Tampa and Jacksonville also offer bus networks. However, public transport may not reach more remote areas, so it's ideal for city travel.

- **Taxis, Rideshares, and Shuttles:** Taxis and rideshare services like Uber and Lyft are widely available in urban areas and airports. Many hotels and resorts also provide shuttle services to popular destinations, particularly tourist-heavy areas.

- **Boats and Ferries:** With its extensive coastline, Florida is home to ferries connecting key islands, such as the Miami-to-Key West ferry. Water taxis are also popular in cities like Fort Lauderdale and Naples.

FLORIDA'S BEACHES AND COASTAL ESCAPES

The Gulf Coast

The Gulf Coast of Florida is a paradise known for its peaceful beaches, crystal-clear waters, and breathtaking sunsets. Stretching along the western edge of the state, this coastal region combines natural beauty with a laid-back atmosphere, offering a perfect escape for beach lovers and outdoor enthusiasts.

1. The Beaches: Florida's Best Shores

The Gulf Coast is home to some of the most beautiful beaches in the U.S., each offering a unique charm:

- **Sanibel Island:** Renowned for its abundant seashells, this quiet island provides a serene, nature-filled experience.

- **Siesta Key:** Famous for its 99% pure quartz sand, this beach often tops global rankings for its soft, powdery shores.

- **Clearwater Beach:** Vibrant and bustling, this beach is perfect for those seeking relaxation and excitement.

- **Fort Myers Beach:** A delightful mix of lively resorts and peaceful retreats, it offers something for every type of visitor.

2. Scenic Sunsets: A Must-See Experience

Watching the sunset over the Gulf is an iconic experience. The stunning views transform the sky into a canvas of brilliant colors. Notable spots for sunset watching include:

- **Pier 60, Clearwater:** A lively location with street performers and local vendors, perfect for enjoying the sunset with a lively atmosphere.

- **Fort Myers Beach:** With many beachfront restaurants offering sunset views, this spot provides an unforgettable dining experience as the sun dips below the horizon.

- **Naples and Destin:** Both locations are renowned for their picturesque sunsets that offer an incredible, tranquil end to the day.

3. Outdoor Adventures and Nature

Beyond the beaches, the Gulf Coast is a haven for nature lovers:

- **J.N. "Ding" Darling National Wildlife Refuge (Sanibel Island):** A premier spot for birdwatching, kayaking, and exploring nature trails.

- **Everglades National Park (Naples):** One of the world's most unique ecosystems, offering airboat rides, wildlife sightings, and swamp tours.

With its stunning beaches, unforgettable sunsets, and outdoor adventures, the Gulf Coast is a must-visit destination that embodies Florida's natural charm and beauty.

The Atlantic Coast

Florida's Atlantic Coast is a paradise for adventure lovers, offering a perfect blend of stunning beaches, outdoor activities, and unforgettable sunrises. From the shores of Jacksonville to the southern tip of Miami, this region is a dynamic playground for travelers seeking relaxation and thrills.

Surfing Hotspots:
The Atlantic Coast is renowned for its surf-friendly beaches, with Jacksonville Beach and Cocoa Beach standing out as top destinations. Jacksonville's north-facing coast catches ideal waves, making it a surfer's dream, while Cocoa Beach, home to the iconic Ron Jon Surf Shop, is perfect for beginners and seasoned surfers. With year-round waves, these areas offer lessons and rentals, so you can easily dive into the action.

Epic Sunrises:
One of the best ways to start your day on Florida's Atlantic Coast is to witness a breathtaking sunrise. The east-facing shores provide a front-row seat to the sun rising over the Atlantic Ocean. Locations like Daytona Beach and Flagler Beach offer expansive views, while the peaceful atmosphere makes for a calming start to your day. For a truly memorable experience, head to the Cape Canaveral National Seashore, where the sight of the sun emerging from the ocean is nothing short of magical.

Outdoor Adventures:
Beyond surfing and sunrises, the Atlantic Coast offers a variety of outdoor adventures. The Everglades National Park is just a short drive from Miami, offering kayaking and wildlife watching. For a more tranquil experience, explore the scenic coastal trails at Anastasia State Park near St. Augustine, known for its pristine beaches and diverse wildlife. Nature lovers will also find rich ecosystems at the Merritt Island Wildlife Refuge and the Canaveral National Seashore.

ORLANDO AND THEME PARK MAGIC

Walt Disney World

Walt Disney World, located in Orlando, is the pinnacle of family-friendly entertainment and magical experiences. Spanning over 25,000 acres, it's more than just a theme park,it is a world of adventure, imagination, and unforgettable memories. Walt Disney World in Orlando continues to innovate, offering new attractions and experiences that keep visitors coming back. In 2025, the magic is even greater with exciting additions across the parks.

The Four Iconic Parks:
- **Magic Kingdom:** The heart of Disney magic, featuring Cinderella's Castle, thrilling rides like Space Mountain, and beloved characters parading down Main Street, U.S.A.

- **Epcot:** A celebration of technology and world cultures, with attractions like Spaceship Earth and World Showcase pavilions highlighting cuisine and traditions from 11 countries.

- **Disney's Hollywood Studios:** Perfect for movie enthusiasts, featuring Star Wars: Galaxy's Edge, Toy Story Land, and classic attractions like The Twilight Zone Tower of Terror.

- **Animal Kingdom:** A unique mix of adventure and wildlife, with highlights like Pandora – The World of Avatar and the thrilling Expedition Everest ride.

New Attractions and Rides:
- **Epcot's Journey to the Stars:** This immersive space-themed ride combines storytelling and cutting-edge technology to take visitors on a galactic adventure.

- **Magic Kingdom's Villains Land:** A highly anticipated new area dedicated to Disney's most infamous villains, featuring thrilling rides, character meet-and-greets, and themed dining experiences.

Enhanced Park Experiences:
- **Genie+ Upgrades:** Disney's revamped Genie+ offers more personalized itineraries, shorter wait times, and enhanced augmented reality features for interactive park navigation.

- **Nighttime Spectaculars:** New fireworks and drone shows light up the skies, including a revamped "Happily Ever After" at Magic Kingdom and "Harmonious 2.0" at Epcot.

Dining and Accommodations:
- **Tiana's Palace Restaurant:** Located in Magic Kingdom, this New Orleans-inspired eatery offers authentic Creole cuisine.

- **Walt Disney World Swan Reserve:** Open to everyone, this luxurious, modern property near EPCOT and Disney's Hollywood Studios offers stunning views, spacious rooms, and fantastic amenities, including complimentary park transportation.

Seasonal Celebrations:
- Disney's 2025 celebrations feature enhanced holiday events, including expanded Halloween and Christmas-themed festivities, making every season magical.

Universal Orlando: Thrills and Innovations

Universal Orlando Resort continues to push the boundaries of entertainment, blending thrilling attractions with cutting-edge technology. In 2025, the resort will introduce new experiences that will captivate visitors of all ages.

New Attractions and Rides:
- **Epic Universe:** Universal's much-anticipated new theme park debuts in 2025, offering immersive lands themed around beloved franchises. Highlights include Super Nintendo World, where guests can explore the Mushroom Kingdom and experience rides like Mario Kart: Bowser's Challenge.

- **Minion Land Expansion:** Universal Studios Florida enhances its Despicable Me offerings with a new interactive attraction, "Villain-Con Minion Blast," and themed dining options like the Minion Cafe.

Enhanced Experiences:
- **Virtual Line Upgrades:** Universal's updated Virtual Line system streamlines ride reservations, reducing wait times and improving guest convenience.

- **New Nighttime Spectacular:** A dazzling projection and fireworks show will debut at Universal's Islands of Adventure, featuring fan-favorite characters and stunning visuals.

Dining and Accommodations:
- **Universal's Endless Summer Resort – Surfside Inn and Suites:** A budget-friendly option offering family suites, beach-inspired decor, and easy access to the parks.

- **New Themed Restaurants:** Discover immersive dining at Epic Universe, including a Yoshi's Island-themed restaurant and other culinary adventures.

Universal Orlando in 2025 promises adrenaline-pumping thrills, family-friendly fun, and unforgettable innovations that elevate the park experience to new heights.

Lesser-Known Theme Parks and Attractions

Florida is home to iconic theme parks, but the lesser-known attractions offer unique experiences without the crowds. The following are some hidden gems worth exploring:

1. Legoland Florida Resort
Location: 1 Legoland Way, Winter Haven, FL 33884,

Located in Winter Haven, Legoland is perfect for families with younger children. The park features Lego-themed rides, interactive exhibits, and impressive Lego sculptures, providing a fun and imaginative atmosphere.

2. Gatorland:
Location: 14501 Orange Blossom Trl, Orlando, FL 32837,

Dubbed the "Alligator Capital of the World," Gatorland in Orlando offers thrilling encounters with alligators and crocodiles. Visitors can watch live shows, feed animals, or even try the "Gator Gauntlet" zipline over crocodile-infested waters.

3. Cypress Gardens Adventure Park
Location: 6000 Cypress Gardens Blvd, Winter Haven, Florida 33884

Although now part of Legoland, Cypress Gardens, located in Winter Haven, is still home to beautiful botanical gardens, old-fashioned water ski shows, and thrilling rides, blending nature and excitement.

4. The Dinosaur World
Location: 5145 Harvey Tew Road, Plant City, FL 33565

Located in Plant City, Dinosaur World is a family-friendly park with life-sized dinosaur sculptures, fossil digging, and educational exhibits. It's a fun and interactive way to learn about prehistoric creatures.

5. WonderWorks
Location: 9067 International Dr, Orlando, FL 32819

Situated in Orlando, WonderWorks is an interactive science museum housed in an upside-down building. It features over 100 exhibits, including optical illusions, virtual reality, and physical challenges.

WILDLIFE AND NATURE ADVENTURES

The Everglades: A UNESCO World Heritage Site

The Everglades, Florida's unique and ecologically significant wetland, is a UNESCO World Heritage Site known for its diverse ecosystems and wildlife.

Unmatched Biodiversity:
Home to rare species like the American crocodile and the West Indian manatee, the Everglades is a haven for wildlife enthusiasts. The park's extensive network of wetlands, sawgrass marshes, and mangroves hosts over 350 bird species, including the endangered wood stork and the roseate spoonbill.

Everglades National Park:
As the largest subtropical wilderness in the U.S., Everglades National Park offers visitors an opportunity to explore a pristine environment. Popular activities include airboat tours, bird watching, and hiking along trails like the Anhinga Trail and Gumbo Limbo Trail, where visitors can observe alligators and other wildlife up close.

Preserving the Ecosystem:
Recognized for its ecological importance, the Everglades has faced challenges from climate change and human activity. Ongoing conservation efforts aim to restore the region's hydrology, ensuring this world heritage site thrives for future generations.

State Parks and Scenic Trails

Florida's state parks and scenic trails offer an incredible way to explore the state's natural beauty, from lush forests to coastal wetlands. Whether you enjoy hiking, wildlife watching, or simply soaking in the scenery, there's something for every adventurer.

1. Topsail Hill Preserve State Park:
Location: 7525 W County Hwy 30A, Santa Rosa Beach, FL 32459

Located on Florida's Gulf Coast, this park features sugar-white beaches, dunes, and freshwater lakes. Enjoy hiking the scenic trails or biking along the picturesque coastline.

2. Black Bear Wilderness Loop Trail:

Location: 5298 Michigan Ave, Sanford, FL 32771

Near Sanford, this 7.1-mile trail weaves through swamps, wetlands, and dense woods, providing an immersive experience of Florida's wild side. It's perfect for wildlife enthusiasts, with opportunities to spot otters, deer, and birds.

3. Myakka River State Park:

Location: 13208 State Road 72, Sarasota, Florida 34241

One of Florida's oldest and largest state parks, Myakka offers hiking trails, wildlife viewing, and a chance to see alligators along the riverbanks. The canopy walkway provides stunning views of the park's diverse ecosystem.

4. Big Cypress National Preserve:

Location: 33100 Tamiami Trail E, Ochopee, Florida 34141

This vast, subtropical preserve offers endless opportunities for exploration, including swamp tours, wildlife viewing, and scenic hikes. Visitors can experience the Everglades' unique ecosystem with a variety of trails, such as the popular Oasis Visitor Center Trail.

5. Tallahassee-St. Marks Historic Railroad Trail:

Location: 4778 Woodville Hwy, Tallahassee, FL 32305

This 16-mile trail stretches from Tallahassee to St. Marks and offers a peaceful journey through scenic forests and along the beautiful Wakulla River. It's a great spot for walking, biking, and wildlife watching.

Florida's Unique Wildlife

Florida is a wildlife enthusiast's dream, home to diverse ecosystems that support unique and fascinating species. From serene waterways to sprawling wetlands, the Sunshine State offers endless opportunities to encounter its iconic wildlife.

1. Manatees: Gentle Giants of Florida:
Known as "sea cows," manatees are a must-see for wildlife lovers. Crystal River and Blue Spring State Park are two of the best spots to observe these gentle giants, especially during winter when they seek warmer waters. You can kayak, paddleboard, or even snorkel alongside them for an unforgettable experience.

2. Alligators: Kings of the Wetlands:
Florida's wetlands are the natural habitat for alligators. Explore the Everglades National Park or take an airboat tour to safely spot these apex predators in their environment. The St. Augustine Alligator Farm also provides an educational and safe way to see them up close.

3. Birdwatching Paradise:
Florida's diverse birdlife includes roseate spoonbills, sandhill cranes, and bald eagles. Merritt Island National Wildlife Refuge and Corkscrew

Swamp Sanctuary are top spots for birdwatching, where you can admire colorful species in pristine habitats.

4. Sea Turtles and Coastal Life:
The Atlantic Coast beaches, especially during nesting season, are hotspots for loggerhead and green sea turtles. Conservation programs offer guided turtle walks to observe nesting habits.

5. Unique Habitats and Rare Species:
Explore the Florida Keys for marine life like dolphins and coral reefs, or visit Ocala National Forest to see black bears and scrub jays. Florida's biodiversity ensures an adventure at every turn.

CITY HIGHLIGHTS

Miami

Art Deco Wonders in South Beach:
Miami's South Beach is a living gallery of Art Deco architecture. Stroll along Ocean Drive to admire pastel-hued buildings with sleek, geometric designs and neon lights. The Art Deco Historic District offers guided tours for those wanting to delve deeper into the 1930s and 1940s architectural styles that define the area.

Vibrant Nightlife and Entertainment:
Miami is synonymous with world-class nightlife. Start your evening at rooftop bars like Juvia or Sugar for stunning city views. Dance the night away in legendary clubs such as LIV at Fontainebleau or STORY. For a more relaxed vibe, Wynwood's eclectic bars and breweries are perfect for cocktails and craft beers.

Cultural Hotspots and Diversity:
Miami's cultural scene reflects its rich diversity. Explore Little Havana, where Cuban culture thrives through live music, hand-rolled cigars, and authentic cuisine at spots like Versailles. In Wynwood, street art and galleries showcase cutting-edge creativity, while the Pérez Art Museum Miami highlights modern and contemporary works.

Shopping and Dining:
Miami's culinary scene is unmatched, blending Latin, Caribbean, and international flavors. Explore high-end shopping at the Design District or discover eclectic finds in Coconut Grove.

Tampa Bay

Tampa Bay, a vibrant region on Florida's Gulf Coast, is a melting pot of rich culture, thrilling attractions, and stunning coastal beauty. It's an ideal destination for travelers seeking urban excitement and seaside serenity.

Cultural Hotspots:
Tampa Bay boasts a thriving arts and culture scene. Visit the Tampa Museum of Art, featuring contemporary works and Greek antiquities, or explore the Salvador Dalí Museum in nearby St. Petersburg, home to the world's largest Dalí collection outside Europe. For history lovers, the Ybor City Historic District offers a deep dive into Tampa's Cuban heritage, with cigar shops, historic buildings, and vibrant nightlife.

Family-Friendly Attractions:
Families flock to Busch Gardens Tampa Bay, a theme park that blends thrilling rides and animal encounters. The Florida Aquarium is another must-visit, offering interactive exhibits and opportunities to learn about marine life.

Outdoor Adventures and Beaches:
Tampa Bay is surrounded by natural beauty. Relax on the soft sands of Clearwater Beach or take a kayak through the mangroves of Weedon Island Preserve. For sports enthusiasts, enjoy fishing, paddleboarding, or attending a Tampa Bay Buccaneers or Rays game.

Dining and Nightlife:
The culinary scene is diverse, with waterfront restaurants serving fresh seafood and craft breweries offering locally brewed beer. Don't miss Hyde Park Village for upscale dining and vibrant nightlife.

Jacksonville

Jacksonville, Florida, is a dynamic blend of urban excitement and natural beauty, making it a top destination for all types of travelers. As the largest city by area in the U.S., it offers a mix of beaches, cultural attractions, and outdoor adventures.

Beaches and Waterfront Fun:
Jacksonville boasts over 22 miles of sandy coastline. Jacksonville Beach is perfect for sunbathing, surfing, or fishing from its iconic pier. Neptune and Atlantic Beaches offer quieter, family-friendly vibes. The St. Johns River, winding through the city, provides opportunities for boating, paddleboarding, and scenic river cruises.

Arts, Culture, and History:
Explore the Riverside Arts Market, a vibrant hub for local art, food, and live music. The Cummer Museum of Art & Gardens features impressive art collections and serene riverside gardens. History buffs will love the

Timucuan Ecological and Historic Preserve, which showcases Native American heritage.

Culinary Delights:
Jacksonville's dining scene blends Southern comfort food with modern twists. Don't miss the craft breweries and local seafood spots, such as Safe Harbor Seafood Market.

Outdoor Adventures:
For nature lovers, the Jacksonville Arboretum and Gardens and Kathryn Abbey Hanna Park offer hiking, biking, and wildlife encounters. Golf enthusiasts can enjoy world-class courses like TPC Sawgrass nearby.

Tallahassee

Tallahassee, Florida's capital city, is a hidden gem blending rich history, vibrant culture, and natural beauty. Nestled in the Panhandle, it offers a unique perspective on Florida's charm beyond its beaches.

Historical Landmarks and Museums:
Tallahassee is a history enthusiast's delight. Visit the Florida State Capitol complex, where the old and new capitol buildings stand side by side. The Museum of Florida History showcases exhibits ranging from Native American heritage to the space age. Don't miss Mission San Luis, a reconstructed 17th-century Spanish settlement offering a glimpse into Florida's colonial past.

Outdoor Adventures and Natural Beauty:
Tallahassee's lush landscapes make it perfect for outdoor enthusiasts. Explore Alfred B. Maclay Gardens State Park, famous for its vibrant camellias and azaleas. Hike or bike the trails at Elinor Klapp-Phipps Park or enjoy kayaking and birdwatching at Lake Talquin State Forest.

Education and Culture:
As home to Florida State University (FSU) and Florida A&M University, Tallahassee boasts a youthful energy. Enjoy art exhibits at the FSU Museum of Fine Arts or live performances at the School of Theatre.

Culinary and Nightlife Scene:
Savor Southern-inspired cuisine at local favorites like Kool Beanz Café or indulge in fresh seafood. After dark, head to Midtown or College Town for craft breweries, live music, and a buzzing nightlife atmosphere.

St. Petersburg and Clearwater

St. Petersburg and Clearwater are two vibrant cities along Florida's Gulf Coast, offering a perfect blend of cultural attractions, natural beauty, and laid-back charm.

Beautiful Beaches:
Clearwater Beach, known for its powdery white sand and clear waters, is consistently ranked among the best beaches in the U.S. St. Petersburg's Pass-a-Grille Beach offers a more tranquil escape, with historic charm and stunning sunset views over the Gulf.

Cultural Attractions:
St. Petersburg is home to several world-class museums, including The Dali Museum, featuring an extensive collection of Salvador Dalí's works. The Museum of Fine Arts and the Chihuly Collection showcase art in a variety of styles and mediums. Clearwater offers the Clearwater Marine Aquarium, famous for rescuing and rehabilitating marine animals, including Winter the dolphin.

Outdoor Activities:
Both cities offer ample opportunities for outdoor adventures. Rent bikes or take a stroll along the Pinellas Trail, a scenic route that stretches between the two cities. Fishing, kayaking, and boat tours are popular in both areas, and dolphin sightings are common.

Dining and Nightlife:
St. Petersburg's downtown offers trendy dining spots, craft breweries, and lively bars. Clearwater's Pier 60 is a popular destination for fresh seafood and beachfront entertainment.

Fort Lauderdale

Fort Lauderdale is a vibrant city known for its picturesque waterways, stunning beaches, and a mix of cultural attractions.

Famous Beaches and Waterfronts:
Fort Lauderdale's coastline offers a lively blend of sun, sand, and surf. The main beach, Fort Lauderdale Beach, is perfect for sunbathing and people-watching. For a quieter escape, visit Las Olas Beach or the serene Fort Lauderdale Beach Park. Explore the city's extensive canal system with a water taxi, offering scenic views of luxury yachts and waterfront mansions.

Las Olas Boulevard:
Las Olas Boulevard is Fort Lauderdale's bustling shopping and dining hub. The area features trendy boutiques, art galleries, and top-notch restaurants. Visitors can stroll along this picturesque street while enjoying vibrant cafés and local craft stores.

Cultural Attractions and Museums:
Fort Lauderdale is home to a rich cultural scene. The NSU Art Museum showcases modern and contemporary works, while the Bonnet House Museum & Gardens offers insight into the city's history. For nature lovers, the Butterfly World is a beautiful and peaceful retreat.

Nightlife and Entertainment:
Fort Lauderdale's nightlife scene is lively, with beachside bars, upscale nightclubs, and music venues to explore, especially around the Fort Lauderdale Beach area.

THE FLORIDA KEYS: ISLAND ESCAPES AND ENDLESS ADVENTURE

Introduction to the Florida Keys

The Florida Keys are a unique chain of islands stretching from the southern tip of Florida, offering a laid-back, tropical paradise. This picturesque destination is known for its stunning landscapes, crystal-clear waters, and vibrant coral reefs, making it a haven for outdoor enthusiasts and those seeking tranquility.

Island Overview

The Florida Keys consist of more than 1,000 islands, with Key West being the most famous. Each island offers its charm, from the lively atmosphere of Key West to the peaceful seclusion of smaller islands like Big Pine Key and Marathon.

Activities and Attractions:

The Keys are perfect for water-based activities like snorkeling, diving, and fishing. John Pennekamp Coral Reef State Park, located in Key Largo, is a must-visit for divers. The Overseas Highway, a 113-mile stretch connecting the Keys, provides scenic views of the turquoise waters and access to iconic spots like the southernmost point of the U.S. in Key West.

Culture and History:
The Florida Keys have a rich history, with Key West known for its connection to writer Ernest Hemingway and its colorful, Caribbean-inspired architecture. The islands also boast a relaxed, island-style lifestyle that attracts visitors seeking a more laid-back vacation experience.

Key Islands and Highlights

1. Key Largo:

- **Gateway to the Florida Keys:** Key Largo, the first and largest of the Florida Keys, is a paradise for nature lovers and adventure seekers. Key Largo, located at the northernmost point of the Florida Keys, serves as the gateway to the island chain. Just a short drive from Miami, it is the perfect starting point for exploring the stunning landscapes and crystal-clear waters of the Keys.

- **Diving Capital of the World:** Key Largo is renowned as the "Diving Capital of the World" due to its world-class dive sites. The waters off Key Largo offer some of the best diving experiences, from exploring coral reefs to wreck dives. The famous Spiegel Grove wreck and Molasses Reef are must-see spots for divers of all levels.

- **John Pennekamp Coral Reef State Park:** One of Key Largo's crown jewels, John Pennekamp Coral Reef State Park, is the first underwater park in the U.S. It offers incredible opportunities for snorkeling, scuba diving, and glass-bottom boat tours. Visitors can experience the vibrant coral reefs, diverse marine life, and the iconic Christ of the Abyss statue submerged off the coast.

2. Islamorada: The Sportfishing Capital and Relaxed Island Vibes

Islamorada, often referred to as the "Sportfishing Capital of the World," is a paradise for anglers and those seeking a relaxed island atmosphere. Located in the Florida Keys, this charming village offers the perfect blend of adventure, scenic beauty, and laid-back vibes.

- **Sportfishing and Boating**: Islamorada is renowned for its world-class fishing opportunities, with access to deep-sea and backcountry waters. Whether you're seeking trophy fish like marlin or tarpon, or prefer a peaceful day fishing the flats, local charters provide expert guidance and equipment. The annual Islamorada Fishing Tournament attracts anglers from around the globe.

- **Relaxed Island Atmosphere**: Beyond fishing, Islamorada is known for its serene atmosphere. Stroll along pristine beaches, enjoy a casual seafood meal by the water, or relax at one of the area's boutique hotels. The slow pace and scenic views make it ideal for unwinding.

- **Wildlife and Nature**: Explore the nearby Everglades National Park or take a kayak tour through mangroves, where you can encounter local wildlife, including dolphins and manatees.

3. Marathon:

- **Family-Friendly Activities in Marathon:** Marathon, located in the Florida Keys, is a fantastic destination for families seeking fun and relaxation. The area is home to beautiful, calm beaches perfect for swimming, snorkeling, and sandcastle building. For a more active experience, visit the Marathon Community Park, featuring playgrounds, picnic areas, and sports facilities, ideal for children and adults alike.

- **Turtle Hospital:** A highlight of Marathon is the renowned Turtle Hospital, dedicated to the rehabilitation and release of sea turtles. Take an educational tour to learn about the hospital's efforts in rescuing injured turtles and the conservation work they do. Visitors can see the turtles up close and even participate in feeding sessions during the tour.

- **Dolphin Encounters:** For a magical experience, don't miss the opportunity for dolphin encounters. Several local tour companies offer boat trips that allow you to observe these playful creatures in their natural habitat. Some tours even provide a chance to swim with dolphins, making it an unforgettable experience for families.

4. Big Pine Key & The Lower Keys:

The Lower Keys, with Big Pine Key as its highlight, offers a tranquil escape from the busier areas of the Florida Keys, featuring stunning natural beauty and outdoor adventures.

- **Serenity and Seclusion**: Big Pine Key provides a peaceful atmosphere, perfect for unwinding and enjoying nature. The island is largely untouched, with serene waters, mangrove-lined shores, and abundant wildlife, making it a perfect spot for relaxation and reflection.

- **Bahia Honda State Park:** Known for its picturesque beaches, clear turquoise waters, and extensive nature trails, Bahia Honda State Park is a must-visit. It offers a range of activities, including snorkeling, kayaking, and cycling, as well as spots for picnicking and birdwatching. The park's iconic Old Bahia Honda Bridge offers incredible views, perfect for sunset watching.

- **The Blue Hole:** Located in the National Key Deer Refuge, the Blue Hole is a unique, freshwater pond home to diverse wildlife, including the endangered Key deer. It's a serene spot for wildlife observation and photography, offering a rare glimpse into the region's natural habitat.

The Lower Keys provide an ideal mix of serenity and adventure, making them perfect for nature lovers and outdoor enthusiasts.

Key West

Key West, the southernmost point of the continental United States, is an idyllic island escape known for its rich history, vibrant culture, and stunning natural beauty. With its eclectic blend of historic landmarks, lively streets, and tranquil beaches, Key West offers a unique blend of adventure and relaxation.

Ernest Hemingway Home and Museum

Located in Key West, the Ernest Hemingway Home and Museum offers an intimate glimpse into the life of one of America's most iconic writers. The property is a must-visit for literature lovers and history enthusiasts alike.

- **Historic House Tour:** The house, built in 1851, was Hemingway's residence from 1931 to 1939. It features Mediterranean Revival architecture and lush gardens. The guided tour showcases the rooms where Hemingway wrote many of his famous works, offering fascinating insights into his creative process.

- **The Hemingway Legacy:** Hemingway wrote "A Farewell to Arms," "To Have and Have Not," and other novels while living there. Visitors can learn about his life in Key West, his family, and the influence the island had on his writing.

- **Famous Six-toed Cats:** The museum is home to descendants of Hemingway's original six-toed cats, a beloved part of his legacy. These cats freely roam the property, adding a unique charm to the experience.

- **Gardens and Grounds:** Explore the beautifully maintained gardens, which Hemingway often enjoyed during his time here. The lush landscaping provides a peaceful retreat that reflects the tranquility he sought in Key West.

Visiting the Ernest Hemingway Home and Museum is an enriching experience for those interested in the life and work of this literary legend.

Duval Street

Duval Street in Key West is a vibrant hub for dining, shopping, and nightlife, capturing the essence of island living.

- **Dining Delights:** Duval Street is home to some of the best eateries in Key West, offering a mix of fresh seafood, Caribbean flavors, and casual dining. Don't miss Blue Heaven, known for its laid-back atmosphere and iconic roosters. For fine dining, El Siboney offers delicious Cuban dishes. For a true Key West experience, try a slice at La Trattoria.

- **Unique Shopping:** The street is lined with quirky shops and boutiques, perfect for finding unique souvenirs. Visit Kermit's Key West Key Lime Shoppe for a taste of the famous key lime pie. For local art, stop by The Studios of Key West, showcasing works from local artists.

- **Nightlife and Bars:** As the sun sets, Duval Street comes alive with music and cocktails. Head to Sloppy Joe's bar, a historic bar with live music, or The Green Parrot bar, a dive bar with a lively local scene. Whether you're into relaxed beach bars or high-energy dance floors, Duval Street has it all.

Southernmost Point

The Southernmost Point in the United States, located in Key West, Florida, is a must-visit landmark for any traveler to the Florida Keys. This vibrant spot is not just famous for its geographical significance but also its iconic photo opportunities. Here's why it should be on your list:

- **The Monument:** The Southernmost Point Buoy, painted in bold red and yellow colors, marks the point where you are just 90 miles away from Cuba. This striking landmark has become a symbol of Key West and is one of the most photographed spots in Florida.

- **A Key West Landmark:** Located at the intersection of Whitehead Street and South Street, the monument is easily accessible, making it perfect for a quick visit. It has become a part of the city's identity, attracting visitors from around the world.

- **Perfect for Photos:** Standing at the monument with the ocean in the background creates a memorable picture. It's a fun way to capture your adventure in the Keys and a keepsake for any travel album.

Outdoor Activities

The Florida Keys, an idyllic chain of islands stretching from Key Largo to Key West, offer a treasure trove of outdoor activities amidst stunning natural beauty.

- **Snorkeling and Scuba Diving:** The Keys are renowned for their vibrant coral reefs, making them a top destination for snorkeling and scuba diving. Key Largo's John Pennekamp Coral Reef State Park is a must-visit, offering crystal-clear waters teeming with marine life. Divers can explore shipwrecks and colorful coral gardens in Key West and Islamorada.

- **Fishing**: Known as the "Fishing Capital of the World," the Florida Keys provide abundant opportunities for both deep-sea and fly fishing. Charter a boat for a day of sport fishing or fish from the shore in Key Largo or Marathon.

- **Kayaking and Paddleboarding:** The calm, shallow waters around the Keys are perfect for kayaking and paddleboarding. Explore the mangroves and marine sanctuaries or glide over the turquoise waters in Bahia Honda State Park.

- **Wildlife Watching:** The Keys are a sanctuary for diverse wildlife. Visit the National Key Deer Refuge in Big Pine Key to spot the rare Key deer or head to the Everglades for birdwatching and alligator sightings.

CULTURAL AND HISTORICAL SITES

St. Augustine: The Nation's Oldest City

Rich History and Colonial Heritage:
St. Augustine, founded in 1565, is the oldest continuously inhabited European-established city in the U.S. Its history spans centuries, with Spanish, British, and American influences shaping its character. Explore the Castillo de San Marcos, a 17th-century fort built to protect the city from pirate attacks.

St. George Street:
St. George Street is the heart of historic St. Augustine. This cobblestone street is lined with charming boutiques, cafes, and colonial-era buildings, offering a glimpse into the past.

Flagler College:
Once the Ponce de León Hotel, this architectural gem features stunning Spanish Renaissance design. The college's historic campus offers guided tours of its grand rooms and gardens.

The Lightner Museum:
Housed in a former luxury hotel, this museum showcases decorative arts, fine art, and historic exhibits, offering a deep dive into Florida's past.

Cuban Heritage in Key West

Key West's Cuban heritage is deeply woven into its history and culture, making the island a unique blend of American and Caribbean influences. The island's Cuban roots are visible in its architecture, food, and festivals.

Cuban Influence on Key West's Architecture:
The vibrant colors and colonial-style buildings of Key West reflect its Cuban influence, particularly in areas like Old Town. The island's Spanish-style homes, often with red-tile roofs, were shaped by the Cuban community that settled here in the 19th century.

Cuban Cuisine:
Key West's Cuban-inspired food scene is a must-experience. From Cuban sandwiches and pastelitos (sweet pastries) to ropa vieja (shredded beef), the island's Cuban eateries offer an authentic taste of the Caribbean. Local favorites like El Siboney and La Granja are renowned for their traditional dishes.

The Cuban Memorial Plaza:
Located in the heart of Key West, the Cuban Memorial Plaza honors the Cuban-American community's contributions to the island. This public space showcases statues and plaques commemorating the island's Cuban heritage.

The Hemingway Home and Museum:
Ernest Hemingway's residence in Key West also has ties to the Cuban community. Hemingway's love for Cuba and its influence on his writing is reflected in the memorabilia on display.

Native American History and Archaeological Sites

Florida's rich Native American history is woven into its landscape, with numerous archaeological sites offering insights into the lives of the state's first inhabitants. Key historical and cultural points to explore:

Timucua Tribe and the Timucuan Ecological & Historic Preserve:
Located in Jacksonville, this preserve offers a glimpse into the Timucua people's way of life. Visitors can explore archaeological sites, including shell mounds, as well as learn about the tribe's cultural practices and interactions with early European settlers.

The Crystal River Archaeological State Park:
This site, a National Historic Landmark, is a significant burial ground for Native Americans who lived in the area around 2,000 years ago. It features ancient burial mounds, providing a window into the ceremonial practices of the early indigenous peoples.

The Calusa and Mound Key Archaeological Site:
Accessible by boat, Mound Key in Southwest Florida was the capital of the Calusa tribe. The island is home to shell mounds and other remains, offering an important historical context about the Calusa culture and its complex society.

Big Cypress National Preserve:
A key site for understanding Native American culture, this preserve contains significant archaeological sites, including old hunting grounds used by the Miccosukee and Seminole tribes. Visitors can explore this area on guided tours that highlight the region's indigenous heritage.

OUTDOOR ADVENTURES AND SPORTS

Snorkeling and Diving Hotspots

Florida is a paradise for snorkelers and divers, offering some of the clearest waters and most diverse marine life in the U.S. Whether you're a beginner or an experienced diver, these hotspots along the state's coastline promise unforgettable underwater experiences.

- **Dry Tortugas National Park (Fort Jefferson):** Accessible only by boat or seaplane, this remote park offers pristine snorkeling and diving in crystal-clear waters. The surrounding coral reefs are teeming with marine life, including fish, rays, and colorful corals.

- **Rainbow River (Dunnellon):** Known for its freshwater springs, Rainbow River is a great spot for snorkeling. The crystal-clear waters allow you to observe fish, turtles, and aquatic plants while drifting downstream.

- **West Palm Beach (Blue Heron Bridge):** A favorite among divers, the Blue Heron Bridge offers access to a rich variety of marine life, including seahorses, starfish, and octopuses, just minutes from the shore.

Golfing in the Sunshine

Florida is known for its sunny weather and world-class golf courses, making it a golfer's paradise. With its year-round pleasant climate and diverse range of courses, from coastal greens to lush inland fairways, the Sunshine State offers something for every golfer, whether a seasoned pro or a casual enthusiast.

Top Golf Destinations:
Florida is home to renowned golf destinations like Palm Beach, Naples, and Orlando. Palm Beach boasts some of the most prestigious courses, such as PGA National Resort & Spa. Naples, known for its upscale lifestyle, offers courses like Tiburón Golf Club. Orlando, with its family-friendly appeal, has fantastic courses like the Waldorf Astoria Golf Club.

Courses with Scenic Views:
Florida's coastal courses offer scenic views, including the renowned Bay Hill Club & Lodge in Orlando, which overlooks the stunning Butler Chain of Lakes. The Links Course at Sandestin Golf & Beach Resort is another gem with picturesque views of the Gulf of Mexico.

Golfing for All Levels:
Whether you're a beginner or an expert, Florida offers a variety of courses that cater to all skill levels. Many resorts also offer lessons and clinics for those looking to improve their game.

State Kayaking, Paddleboarding, and Fishing

Florida's waterways are ideal for outdoor sports, offering a variety of experiences for adventure lovers. Whether you're gliding through mangroves or casting a line in the open sea, these activities promise a memorable adventure.

Kayaking in Florida:
Kayaking in Florida is a must-do for nature enthusiasts. Explore the Everglades, home to diverse wildlife, or paddle through the crystal-clear waters of the Florida Keys. The Wekiva River and the Blackwater Creek offer peaceful paddles through lush landscapes, while the swift currents of the Apalachicola River challenge experienced kayakers.

Paddleboarding:
Paddleboarding is another popular water sport in Florida, ideal for a leisurely exploration or a fun workout. The calm waters of Sarasota's beaches are perfect for beginners, while more experienced paddleboarders can challenge themselves in places like Key Biscayne or the Indian River Lagoon.

Fishing Adventures:
Florida is known for its world-class fishing. From deep-sea fishing in the Gulf to catching bass in freshwater lakes, the state offers numerous fishing opportunities. Head to the Florida Keys for saltwater fishing or to Lake Okeechobee for some of the best bass fishing in the country.

FOOD AND DRINK IN FLORIDA

Iconic Dishes

Florida's culinary scene is as diverse as its culture, offering a mix of fresh seafood, Latin influences, and Southern comfort. Here are some of the must-try iconic dishes that define Florida's food culture.

1. Cuban Sandwich: A beloved Florida staple, the Cuban sandwich features roast pork, ham, Swiss cheese, pickles, and mustard, all pressed between Cuban bread. It's especially popular in Miami and Tampa, where local variations add unique touches.

2. Key Lime Pie: No trip to Florida is complete without a slice of Key Lime Pie. This tangy, creamy dessert made with key lime juice, sweetened condensed milk, and a graham cracker crust is a true taste of the Florida Keys.

3. Stone Crab Claws: Known for their sweet, tender meat, stone crab claws are a seasonal delicacy in Florida, typically served cold with mustard sauce. Key West is a popular spot to try them.

4. Conch Fritters: A Caribbean-inspired dish, conch fritters are deep-fried balls of conch meat, seasoned with spices, and served with dipping sauce. These savory snacks are found in many coastal towns.

5. Fried Grouper: Grouper, a firm white fish, is a Florida favorite often served fried or grilled. It's featured prominently in coastal restaurants across the state.

6. Fried Gator: For a unique Florida experience, try fried alligator. Typically served as an appetizer, this dish offers a tender, mild flavor with a crispy coating.

Florida's Culinary Scene

Seafood: Fresh from the Gulf and Atlantic
Florida is famous for its seafood, with dishes like stone crab, grouper, and mahi-mahi featuring prominently on menus. In cities like Miami and Key West, you'll find a variety of seafood shacks offering freshly caught fish and shrimp. Don't miss the iconic Cuban sandwich, a Florida favorite, filled with roast pork, ham, pickles, and mustard.

Food Trucks: Flavor on the Go
The state's vibrant food truck scene is a true representation of Florida's diverse culinary influences. From tacos in Tampa to gourmet bites in Orlando, food trucks are a popular option for a quick but delicious meal. Try Cuban sandwiches, fresh ceviche, or savory empanadas as you explore the bustling street food markets.

Fine Dining and International Cuisine:
For those looking for a refined dining experience, Florida offers a range of high-end restaurants. Miami's South Beach is home to a variety of Michelin-starred spots, serving contemporary American, Italian, and fusion cuisines. You can also enjoy authentic Latin and Caribbean dishes in cities like Miami and Tampa, where diverse communities influence the flavors.

Local Drinks

Florida's food and drink scene is as vibrant and diverse as its landscape. The state is known for its unique beverages, from refreshing craft beers to rum concoctions that evoke tropical vibes. Here's a look at some must-try local drinks.

- **Craft Beer:** Florida's craft beer scene has exploded in recent years, with breweries scattered across the state. Miami, Tampa, and St. Petersburg lead the charge, offering innovative brews ranging from tropical IPAs to rich stouts. Key West's The Florida Keys Brewing Company and Tampa's Cigar City Brewing are top spots for beer enthusiasts to sample local flavors.

- **Citrus Wines:** Florida is well known for its production of citrus, particularly oranges. Local vineyards are now experimenting with citrus wines, creating a unique blend of sweet and tart flavors. The Citrus Tower Winery, located in Clermont, offers wines made from Florida-grown fruits like oranges and grapefruits, providing a refreshing alternative to traditional grape wines.

- **Rum Distilleries:** Rum is Florida's signature spirit, and the state's distilleries produce some of the finest. The Key West Distillery and St. Augustine Distillery are popular choices, offering tours and tastings of locally crafted rum. These distilleries incorporate tropical fruits like mango and coconut into their blends, giving their spirits a distinctive Florida flair.

Restaurants in Florida

Here are five must-visit restaurants that showcase the best of the Sunshine State's vibrant food culture.

1. Joe's Stone Crab:
Location: 11 Washington Ave, Miami Beach, FL 33139

An iconic Miami Beach institution, Joe's Stone Crab is famous for its fresh stone crabs served with mustard sauce. It's a classic spot for seafood lovers, offering a wide variety of dishes like shrimp cocktails, lobster, and their signature stone crab.

2. Bern's Steak House:

Location: 1208 S Howard Ave, Tampa, FL 33606

Renowned for its high-quality steaks and impeccable service, Bern's Steak House in Tampa is a Florida classic. Known for its dry-aged beef and expansive wine list, Bern's offers a timeless dining experience, complete with a dessert room.

3. The Capital Grille:

Location: 2430 E Sunrise Blvd, Fort Lauderdale, FL 33304

This upscale chain restaurant is known for its expertly cooked steaks, fresh seafood, and elegant atmosphere. The Fort Lauderdale location is a favorite for special occasions and business dinners.

4. The Surf Club Restaurant:

Location: 9011 Collins Ave, Surfside, FL 33154

Located in the historic Surf Club, this Michelin-starred restaurant by Thomas Keller offers an elegant menu with a mix of seafood, prime steaks, and an exceptional wine selection.

5. Yardbird Southern Table & Bar:

Location: 1600 Lenox Ave., Miami Beach, FL 33139

Offering elevated Southern comfort food, Yardbird is known for its fried chicken, biscuits, and classic Southern sides. It's a favorite for those looking for a down-home yet refined dining experience.

SHOPPING AND SOUVENIRS

Best Shopping Destinations

Florida is a shopper's paradise, offering everything from sprawling malls to unique markets and charming boutiques. Whether you're hunting for luxury items, quirky souvenirs, or locally made goods, Florida's shopping destinations cater to every taste.

World-Class Malls:

1. The Mall at Millenia:
Location: 4200 Conroy Rd, Orlando, FL 32839

This upscale mall features high-end brands like Gucci, Louis Vuitton, and Chanel, alongside department stores like Macy's and Bloomingdale's.

2 Aventura Mall:
Location: 19501 Biscayne Blvd, Aventura, FL 33180

One of the largest malls in Florida, it boasts over 300 stores, a mix of luxury and mid-range brands, and an impressive art collection.

3. International Plaza and Bay Street:
Location: 2223 N Westshore Blvd, Tampa, Florida 33607

A blend of luxury shopping, dining, and entertainment, this stylish destination features high-end retailers like Nordstrom and Neiman Marcus, alongside trendy restaurants.

Vibrant Markets:

- **Miami's Bayside Marketplace**: A lively outdoor market offering waterfront shopping, souvenirs, and live music.

- **St. Petersburg's Saturday Morning Market**: Known for handmade crafts, artisanal foods, and fresh produce, this market reflects local creativity.

- **Red Barn Flea Market in Bradenton**: This market offers a mix of over 600 flea market booths and shops, providing a variety of goods from fresh produce to unique collectibles.

Charming Boutiques:

- **Worth Avenue, Palm Beach:** A sophisticated shopping district lined with high-end boutiques, designer stores, and chic cafes.

- **Las Olas Boulevard, Fort Lauderdale:** A hotspot for stylish boutiques, art galleries, and unique gifts.

- **Historic St. George Street, St. Augustine:** Quaint shops offering local crafts, jewelry, and souvenirs in a picturesque historic setting.

Florida's shopping destinations aren't just about retail, they are experiences that combine culture, luxury, and local charm. Whether strolling through a high-end mall or exploring a bustling market, each venue promises something special.

Unique Florida Souvenirs

Florida offers a variety of distinctive souvenirs that reflect the state's vibrant culture, natural beauty, and coastal charm. Here are some must-have items to bring home from your Sunshine State adventure:

- **Key Lime Treats:** A true taste of Florida, key lime pies and candies are iconic souvenirs. Grab a jar of key lime pie filling, key lime cookies, or preserves to share the tangy, tropical flavor.

- **Sea Shells and Coral Art:** Florida's coastal shops feature stunning seashells and coral crafts. From handmade jewelry to decorative pieces, these souvenirs bring a touch of the ocean into your home.

- **Citrus-Inspired Products:** Florida is famous for its oranges, and citrus-inspired souvenirs abound. Look for orange-scented candles, jams, marmalades, and fresh citrus fruit baskets.

- **Everglades and Wildlife-Themed Items:** Explore unique gifts inspired by Florida's natural landscapes, such as alligator leather goods, Everglades-themed artwork, or eco-friendly wildlife plush toys for kids.

- **Local Art and Crafts:** Support local artists by purchasing handcrafted pottery, paintings, or jewelry that capture Florida's colorful essence.

- **Theme Park Exclusives:** Bring home exclusive merchandise from Walt Disney World, Universal Studios, or other theme parks for a fun, nostalgic keepsake.

Outlet Shopping Tips

Florida is a shopper's paradise, and its outlet malls offer incredible deals on high-quality brands. To make the most of your outlet shopping experience, follow these tips:

1. Choose the Best Outlets: Florida has some of the country's top outlet malls. Visit Sawgrass Mills in Sunrise, one of the largest in the U.S., or Orlando International Premium Outlets, a favorite for Disney visitors. For a luxurious shopping experience, head to Tampa Premium Outlets or St. Augustine Outlets for upscale brands at discounted prices.

2. Shop Smart with a Plan: Before visiting, research the outlet's store directory online to prioritize your favorite brands. Arrive on time to avoid crowds and get the best deals. Bring a reusable shopping bag to carry your finds conveniently.

3. Look for Discounts and Promotions: Many outlets offer additional discounts through their websites, apps, or loyalty programs. Sign up for these to receive extra savings and exclusive coupons.

4. Dress Comfortably: Wear comfortable clothing and shoes, as outlet malls can be expansive. Carry a water bottle to stay hydrated while browsing.

5. Timing is Key: Weekdays and mornings are less crowded, offering a more relaxed shopping experience. Visit during holiday sales for deeper discounts.

ACCOMMODATIONS IN FLORIDA

Luxury Resorts and Hotels

Florida is home to some of the most opulent resorts and hotels, offering unmatched luxury, world-class amenities, and breathtaking surroundings. Here are six standout options:

1. The Breakers:
Location: 1 S County Rd, Palm Beach, FL 33480

A historic icon of luxury, The Breakers offers oceanfront rooms, a private beach, championship golf courses, and award-winning dining. The Mediterranean-inspired architecture adds to its timeless charm.

2. Acqualina Resort & Residences:
Location: 17875 Collins Ave, Sunny Isles Beach, FL 33160

This Forbes Five-Star resort boasts Mediterranean-style luxury, private beachfront access, world-class spa services, and gourmet dining options.

3. The Ritz-Carlton:
Location: 2600 Tiburon Dr, Naples, FL 34109

Situated along the Gulf of Mexico, this resort offers serene beachfront luxury, fine dining, a rejuvenating spa, and two golf courses for a perfect retreat.

4. Faena Hotel:
Location: 3201 Collins Ave, Miami Beach, Florida 33140

Known for its bold design and artistic flair, Faena Hotel features luxurious oceanfront rooms, a world-class theater, and innovative dining experiences.

5. Amara Cay Resort:
Location: 80001 Overseas Hwy, Islamorada, Florida 33036

A hidden gem in the Florida Keys, this resort offers a tranquil escape with private beaches, water sports, and spectacular ocean views.

6. The Don CeSar:
Location: 3400 Gulf Blvd, St Pete Beach, Florida 33706

Known as the "Pink Palace," this historic beachfront hotel combines luxury and history. With its iconic pink exterior and lavish amenities, guests enjoy oceanfront views, fine dining, and world-class spa services.

Budget-Friendly Options

Traveling to Florida doesn't have to break the bank. From beachside motels to affordable inns, here are six budget-friendly accommodations for travelers looking to save without compromising comfort.

1. Quality Inn & Suites by the Parks:
Location: 2945 Entry Point Blvd, Kissimmee, FL 34747

Located near Orlando's theme parks, this affordable hotel offers clean rooms, free breakfast, and a complimentary shuttle to Walt Disney World.

2. Sun Dek Beach House
Location: 6666 N Ocean Blvd, Boynton Beach, FL 33435

This boutique property offers budget-friendly accommodations with easy access to the Atlantic Ocean. Guests enjoy kitchenettes, lush gardens, and a pool.

3. The Flamingo Hotel and Tower
Location: 15525 Front Beach Rd, Panama City Beach, FL 32413, United States

A classic beachside hotel with affordable rates, The Flamingo Hotel and Tower is ideal for travelers looking to soak up the sun on Florida's Panhandle.

4. La Quinta Inn by Wyndham
Location: 908 NW 69th Terrace, Gainesville, FL 32605

Offering clean rooms, free breakfast, and a central location, this property is a convenient stop for those exploring North Florida.

5. Tropical Winds Oceanfront Hotel
Location: 1398 N Atlantic Ave, Daytona Beach, Florida 32118

This budget-friendly hotel offers oceanfront rooms with kitchenettes, an indoor and outdoor pool, and direct beach access. Its central location makes it a great option for travelers visiting Daytona Beach on a budget.

6. Key West Hospitality Inns

For those visiting the Keys, this budget option provides simple accommodations with great access to Key West's attractions and nightlife.

Unique Stays

Florida offers an array of unique accommodations, from historic inns to eco-friendly retreats, each providing an unforgettable experience. Here are six distinctive places to stay:

1. Jules Undersea Lodge
Location: 51 Shoreland Dr, Key Largo, Florida 33037

For a truly unique experience, stay at this underwater lodge. Accessible only by scuba diving, it offers a one-of-a-kind opportunity to sleep surrounded by marine life in a submerged habitat.

2. St. Francis Inn Bed and Breakfast
Location: 279 St George St, St. Augustine, FL 32084

This historic bed-and-breakfast blends old-world charm with modern comfort. Dating back to 1791, it offers cozy rooms, complimentary breakfast, and proximity to St. Augustine's attractions.

3. Coldwater Gardens Treehouse

Location: 7009 Creek Stone Rd, Milton, FL 32570

Elevate your nature experience in this privately located treehouse situated among a dense magnolia canopy. All enclosed rooms have heat and AC, providing comfort amidst nature.

4. Houseboats at Mangrove Marina

Location: 200 Florida Ave, Tavernier, FL 33070

Stay in well-appointed houseboats with all the comforts of home, including full kitchens and cozy interiors. Enjoy direct access to water activities like kayaking and paddleboarding in the Florida Keys.

SEASONAL EVENTS AND FESTIVALS

Music Festivals: From EDM to Jazz

Florida's music festival scene is a vibrant mix of genres, offering something for every music lover. Whether you're into the energetic beats of EDM or the smooth rhythms of jazz, Florida hosts world-renowned festivals throughout the year.

EDM Festivals:
Florida is a hotspot for electronic dance music (EDM) lovers, with festivals like the Ultra Music Festival in Miami, which is one of the biggest and most famous EDM events in the world. With top DJs spinning electrifying sets, it's a must-attend for dance music enthusiasts. Sunset Music Festival in Tampa and Electric Daisy Carnival in Orlando also draw large crowds, offering an immersive experience of lights, music, and high-energy performances.

Jazz Festivals:
For those who appreciate the soulful sounds of jazz, Florida offers incredible festivals like the Jacksonville Jazz Festival, which attracts top-tier jazz artists from around the world. The Miami Beach Jazz Festival and Clearwater Jazz Holiday are also renowned, offering a mix of intimate performances and large-scale events that showcase classic and contemporary jazz.

Diverse Music Celebrations:
Beyond EDM and jazz, Florida is home to numerous other music festivals. The Florida Folk Festival celebrates folk music, while Fort Lauderdale's Las Olas Art Fair combines jazz, art, and culture into a weekend of creative expression.

Art Shows, Parades, and Cultural Events

Florida is a vibrant hub for art and culture, offering a variety of events throughout the year that celebrate creativity, diversity, and tradition.

Art Shows and Festivals:
Florida hosts numerous art shows and festivals, showcasing local and international talent. The Art Basel Miami Beach, one of the world's premier contemporary art fairs, brings cutting-edge works from around the globe. St. Petersburg's annual Mainsail Art Festival is another highlight, featuring over 200 artists in a beautiful outdoor setting.

Parades:
Parades are an essential part of Florida's cultural scene. The Miami Carnival, a lively celebration of Caribbean culture, is one of the largest and most colorful events in the state, with music, dance, and elaborate costumes. The Gasparilla Pirate Festival in Tampa is another iconic parade, where pirates invade the city in a grand procession full of festivities.

Cultural Events and Performances:

Florida's rich cultural diversity is reflected in events such as the Florida Film Festival, showcasing independent films, or the Sarasota Opera, where world-class performances take place. The Florida Folk Festival in White Springs celebrates the state's cultural heritage with music, food, and storytelling, offering a true taste of Florida's traditions.

Sports Events and Tournaments

Florida is a sports lover's paradise, hosting world-class events and tournaments throughout the year. From major league games to unique sporting competitions, the Sunshine State is buzzing with action.

Professional Sports:
Florida is home to several major league teams, including the Miami Dolphins (NFL), Miami Heat (NBA), Orlando Magic (NBA), and Tampa Bay Buccaneers (NFL). You can also catch top-tier baseball with the Miami Marlins (MLB) and the Tampa Bay Rays (MLB). These teams offer unforgettable live sporting experiences.

Tennis – The Miami Open:
One of the biggest tennis events in the U.S., the Miami Open attracts the world's best players. Held annually at Hard Rock Stadium, this prestigious tournament draws thousands of fans for an exciting display of elite tennis.

Auto Racing – Daytona 500:

The Daytona 500 is one of NASCAR's crown jewels, bringing high-speed excitement to the iconic Daytona International Speedway. This race is a must-see for motorsport fans, showcasing intense competition and thrilling finishes.

Golf Tournaments:
Florida is a premier golfing destination, hosting events like the Players Championship in Ponte Vedra Beach, offering a chance to see the best golfers in action.

HIDDEN GEMS IN FLORIDA

Off-the-Beaten-Path Destinations

While Florida is known for its famous beaches and theme parks, it also offers a wealth of hidden gems waiting to be discovered. From serene natural spots to quaint towns, here are some off-the-beaten-path destinations you shouldn't miss.

1. Devil's Den Prehistoric Spring and Campground:
Tucked away in Williston, Devil's Den Spring is a unique prehistoric spring that attracts divers and snorkelers. Its crystal-clear waters, ancient rock formations, and underground cavern make it a one-of-a-kind spot for adventure seekers.

2. St. George Island:
Just off the Gulf Coast, St. George Island is a peaceful retreat with miles of unspoiled beaches, wildlife refuges, and secluded vacation homes. It's perfect for those looking to escape the hustle and bustle and enjoy natural beauty in a serene setting.

3. Devil's Millhopper Geological State Park:
Location: 4732 Millhopper Rd, Gainesville, FL 32653

In Gainesville, this park features a massive sinkhole surrounded by lush, tropical vegetation. Hike down the boardwalks and discover a unique ecosystem filled with ferns, mosses, and hidden springs.

4. The Coral Castle:

Location: 28655 S Dixie Hwy, Homestead, Florida 33033

This mysterious structure was created by a single man, Edward Leedskalnin, over 28 years. The Coral Castle is a fascinating feat of engineering, with large coral stones that seem to defy the laws of physics.

5. Sanibel Island:

Famous for its shell-filled beaches, Sanibel Island is a tranquil alternative to the busy resorts of Southwest Florida. It's a great place for eco-tourism and birdwatching, especially in the J.N. "Ding" Darling National Wildlife Refuge.

6. The Forgotten Coast:

Tucked away on Florida's Panhandle, the Forgotten Coast is a pristine stretch of coastline that remains largely untouched by commercial development. Visit small towns like Apalachicola and Port St. Joe for quiet beaches, charming boutiques, and incredible seafood. It's an ideal spot for those seeking a peaceful retreat away from the crowds.

7. The Crystal River:

Florida's Crystal River is one of the best places to encounter manatees in the wild. This serene river offers a chance to swim alongside these gentle giants, especially during winter when they gather in warm waters.

8. Dry Tortugas National Park:

Accessible only by boat or seaplane, Dry Tortugas is a remote island paradise with white-sand beaches, vibrant coral reefs, and the historic Fort Jefferson. It's a perfect spot for snorkeling, history buffs, and nature lovers.

Underrated Small Towns

Florida is home to charming small towns that offer a more peaceful, authentic experience. These hidden gems provide a unique glimpse into Florida's local culture, history, and natural beauty.

1. Mount Dora:
Nestled on the shores of Lake Dora, this quaint town is known for its historic downtown filled with antique shops, cozy cafes, and scenic lakeside views. It's the perfect place for a relaxing weekend getaway, with art festivals, boat tours, and charming bed-and-breakfasts.

2. Cedar Key:
A quiet coastal village, Cedar Key is an untouched paradise for seafood lovers and nature enthusiasts. With its small-town vibe, the town offers excellent opportunities for kayaking, birdwatching, and fishing. The stunning sunsets and historic architecture provide a relaxing backdrop to a laid-back Florida experience.

3. Micanopy:
Located just outside Gainesville, Micanopy is known for its old-fashioned charm and historic buildings. Stroll through its antique shops, explore local history, and enjoy the natural beauty of nearby Paynes Prairie Preserve State Park.

4. Apalachicola:
A charming Gulf Coast town, Apalachicola offers a rich history, great seafood, and beautiful waterfront views. Its well-preserved Victorian architecture and proximity to pristine beaches make it an ideal off-the-beaten-path destination.

SCENIC DRIVES AND ROAD TRIP ROUTES

The Overseas Highway: A Drive to Remember

Florida's Overseas Highway, commonly referred to as U.S. Route 1, is one of the most famous road trips in the world. Spanning 113 miles and connecting the Florida mainland to Key West, this drive offers breathtaking views, unique stops, and unforgettable experiences.

Spectacular Views of the Ocean:
Driving the Overseas Highway feels like gliding over the sea. The road stretches across 42 bridges, including the famous Seven Mile Bridge, offering panoramic views of turquoise waters and coral reefs. You'll witness endless horizons where the Atlantic Ocean meets the Gulf of Mexico.

Must-Visit Stops Along the Way:
Begin your journey in Key Largo, home to the John Pennekamp Coral Reef State Park, ideal for snorkeling or glass-bottom boat tours. Stop at Islamorada for its world-class sport fishing and the History of Diving Museum. Marathon is a perfect mid-point for family-friendly activities like the Turtle Hospital or Dolphin Research Center.

Key West: The Ultimate Destination:
The journey ends in Key West, the southernmost point of the U.S., known for its vibrant culture, historic landmarks, and lively nightlife. Visit the Ernest Hemingway Home and Museum or catch a sunset celebration at Mallory Square.

A1A Coastal Byway

The A1A Coastal Byway is one of Florida's most iconic scenic drives, stretching along the Atlantic Coast from Amelia Island to Key West. This historic route offers breathtaking coastal views, charming small towns, and a rich mix of natural beauty and cultural landmarks.

1. Amelia Island to St. Augustine:
Starting in Amelia Island, the A1A winds south past pristine beaches and moss-draped oaks. Stop at Fort Clinch State Park, where you can explore 19th-century military history and enjoy scenic trails. Continuing south, make your way to St. Augustine, the oldest city in the U.S., where you can wander through cobblestone streets, visit the Castillo de San Marcos, and enjoy the historic architecture.

2. Flagler Beach and Daytona Beach:
Heading further south, Flagler Beach offers quiet stretches of sand perfect for relaxing. Daytona Beach, known for its speedway, also boasts a vibrant boardwalk and a lively atmosphere, ideal for stopping and soaking up the coastal charm.

3. Cocoa Beach to the Florida Keys:
The A1A leads through iconic beach towns like Cocoa Beach and Vero Beach before reaching the Florida Keys. Key West marks the end of the journey, where you can take in the sunset at Mallory Square and explore the island's vibrant culture.

Historic Tamiami Trail

The Historic Tamiami Trail is one of Florida's most iconic and scenic drives, stretching 275 miles from Miami to Tampa. This route offers travelers a unique glimpse into the state's natural beauty, wildlife, and history.

Route Overview
The Tamiami Trail, officially U.S. Route 41, traverses the southern portion of the state, connecting Miami to the Gulf Coast. It cuts through the heart of the Everglades, offering travelers an unforgettable journey across diverse landscapes, from swamplands to coastal vistas.

Everglades National Park
One of the main highlights of the Tamiami Trail is its proximity to the Everglades National Park. Travelers can stop at several points along the trail to experience the park's unique ecosystem. Take a detour to Shark Valley, where you can spot alligators, birds, and other wildlife.

Big Cypress National Preserve

Heading westward, the Tamiami Trail crosses the Big Cypress National Preserve, a vast area of wetlands. This part of the drive offers numerous opportunities for eco-tourism, including birdwatching, hiking, and wildlife viewing.

Cultural and Historical Stops

Along the way, visitors can explore small historic towns like Ochopee, home to the world's smallest post office, and visit local attractions like the Miccosukee Indian Village.

FLORIDA FOR FAMILIES

Kid-Friendly Attractions

Florida is a family-friendly destination, with an abundance of attractions that offer fun and educational experiences for children of all ages. From theme parks to interactive museums, the state provides countless opportunities for family bonding.

1. Walt Disney World Resort:
No trip to Florida is complete without a visit to the world-renowned Walt Disney World Resort in Orlando. With four theme parks—Magic Kingdom, EPCOT, Disney's Hollywood Studios, and Disney's Animal Kingdom—there's something for every child. Meet beloved characters, enjoy thrilling rides, and immerse yourself in Disney's magical world.

2. Universal Studios Florida:
Location: 6000 Universal Blvd, Orlando, FL 32819

Another popular destination for families is Universal Studios in Orlando, where kids can explore movie-themed attractions like The Wizarding World of Harry Potter, Jurassic Park, and Minions. It's perfect for families with children who enjoy exciting rides and entertainment.

3. SeaWorld Orlando:
Location: 7007 Sea World Dr, Orlando, Florida 32821

For animal lovers, SeaWorld Orlando offers the chance to see marine life up close. Kids can interact with dolphins, watch whale shows, and enjoy thrilling rides like Mako and Kraken.

4. The Florida Aquarium:
Location: Channelside Dr, Tampa, FL 33602

Located in Tampa, The Florida Aquarium is a fun and educational experience. Children can explore over 200 species of aquatic life, including sea turtles, sharks, and stingrays.

5. LEGOLAND Florida Resort:
Situated in Winter Haven, LEGOLAND is perfect for younger children, with interactive attractions and themed rides based on the beloved toy blocks.

Tips for Traveling with Kids

To ensure a smooth and enjoyable trip, here are some essential tips for traveling with kids in the Sunshine State.

- **Plan Ahead for Theme Parks:** Florida is home to world-renowned theme parks like Disney World, Universal Studios, and SeaWorld. To avoid long lines, purchase tickets in advance and take advantage of early entry options. Consider using mobile apps to track ride wait times and map out the park's best attractions for your kids' age group.

- **Pack for Comfort and Convenience:** Florida's hot and humid weather can be intense, so pack lightweight clothing, sunscreen, hats, and plenty of water. If you're visiting theme parks, bring a stroller for younger children to avoid fatigue. Don't forget snacks to keep your energy levels up!

- **Explore Nature and Outdoor Adventures:** Beyond the theme parks, Florida offers plenty of outdoor adventures for families. Take a family-friendly hike in the Everglades or enjoy a wildlife encounter at the Tampa Bay Aquarium. You can also explore Florida's beaches, offering gentle waves perfect for kids to swim and play.

- **Kid-Friendly Accommodation:** Choose family-oriented hotels with amenities like pools, free breakfasts, and kids' clubs. Many resorts cater specifically to families, offering babysitting services, child-sized amenities, and easy access to local attractions.

KID-FRIENDLY ACCOMMODATIONS

Florida is a top family destination, and choosing the right accommodation can make a trip even more enjoyable. Here are six kid-friendly stays that offer comfort, fun, and convenience.

1. Disney's Art of Animation Resort:
Location: 1850 Animation Way, Lake Buena Vista, Florida 32830

This themed resort brings Disney movies to life with family suites inspired by The Lion King, Finding Nemo, and more. The resort features the largest pool at Walt Disney World, interactive play areas, and easy access to the parks via the Skyliner.

2. LEGOLAND Florida Resort:
Location: 1 Legoland Way, Winter Haven, FL 33884

Perfect for LEGO-loving kids, this resort features themed rooms, treasure hunts, and early park access. The on-site water park and nightly entertainment add extra fun for families.

3. Hawks Cay Resort:
Location: 61 Hawks Cay Blvd, Duck Key, Florida 33050

A paradise for families, Hawks Cay offers a kids' club, dolphin encounters, and a pirate ship pool. Parents can enjoy spa treatments while kids take part in outdoor adventures.

4. TradeWinds Island Grand Resort:
Location: 5500 Gulf Blvd, St Pete Beach, Florida 33706

This beachfront resort offers a floating water park, kids' activities, and multiple pools. Families can enjoy beach cabanas, paddleboarding, and themed dining experiences.

5. The Ritz-Carlton Amelia Island:
Location: 4750 Amelia Island Pkwy, Amelia Island, Florida 32034

Combining luxury and kid-friendly amenities, this resort offers a kids' club, nature programs, and pirate-themed activities. The beachfront location ensures endless family fun.

6. The Grove Resort & Water Park Orlando:
Location: 14501 Grove Resort Ave, Winter Garden, Florida 34787

Just minutes from Walt Disney World, this resort features spacious suites, a massive on-site water park with a lazy river and water slides, and a family-friendly arcade. It's an excellent choice for families looking for fun outside the theme parks.

Best Family Beaches

Florida is renowned for its beautiful beaches, many of which are perfect for family vacations. With calm waters, soft sand, and a variety of kid-friendly activities, these beaches offer something for everyone.

Siesta Key Beach:
Located on Florida's Gulf Coast, Siesta Key is famous for its powdery white sand and gentle, shallow waters. It's ideal for young children to play safely in the surf. The beach also has picnic areas and playgrounds, making it a great spot for family gatherings.

Clearwater Beach:

Known for its crystal-clear waters and family-friendly atmosphere, Clearwater Beach on the Gulf Coast has plenty to offer families. Enjoy the wide beach, calm waves, and a lively promenade with restaurants and shops. The nearby Clearwater Marine Aquarium is a must-see for animal lovers.

Destin Beach:

Situated in the Florida Panhandle, Destin is famous for its emerald-green waters and soft white sand. The beach is calm and shallow, perfect for children. Families can enjoy nearby attractions like the Destin Harbor Boardwalk and water parks.

Fort De Soto Park:

This hidden gem in St. Petersburg is ideal for families seeking a more secluded experience. With calm waters, picnic areas, and an extensive bike trail, Fort De Soto Park offers a peaceful retreat for families to explore and relax.

PRACTICAL INFORMATION

Travel Safety in Florida

When exploring Florida, it's important to prioritize safety to ensure a smooth and enjoyable trip. The state offers numerous outdoor activities, but knowing how to stay safe is key to having an unforgettable experience.

- **Weather Precautions:** Florida's tropical climate means sudden weather changes, including thunderstorms and hurricanes. Always check the weather forecast before heading out, especially during the summer months. If you're visiting during hurricane season (June to November), have an emergency plan in place and stay informed about storm warnings.

- **Wildlife Safety:** Florida is home to wildlife, including alligators, snakes, and marine creatures. Never feed animals and stay a safe distance away from them. When kayaking, paddleboarding, or swimming, be mindful of your surroundings, especially in areas known for alligators or jellyfish.

- **Sun Protection:** Florida's sun can be intense, so use sunscreen with a high SPF, wear protective clothing, and stay hydrated. Avoid spending too much time in the sun between (10 a.m. to 4 p.m.) to reduce the risk of heatstroke or sunburn.

- **Driving Safety:** Florida's roads can be busy, particularly in tourist areas. Always obey speed limits and traffic laws. In case of an emergency, have a basic first aid kit and know the locations of the nearest hospitals or clinics.

Weather and Hurricane Season Tips

Florida's weather is as diverse as its landscapes, with sunshine year-round, but it's important to understand its climate and hurricane season to plan your visit accordingly.

Year-Round Sunshine: Florida enjoys a tropical climate, with warm temperatures year-round. Summer (June to September) brings hot and humid weather, especially in southern regions like Miami and the Florida Keys. Winter (December to February) offers mild temperatures, ideal for outdoor activities. Northern Florida can experience cooler temperatures during the winter, but it remains pleasant overall.

Hurricane Season (June to November):
Florida's hurricane season runs from June through November, with the highest risk typically occurring from August to October. Hurricanes can bring heavy rain, strong winds, and coastal flooding, especially along the Gulf Coast and the Atlantic Coast.

Hurricane Preparedness Tips

- **Check Weather Forecasts:** Monitor weather updates, particularly during the summer and fall, to stay informed about potential storms.

- **Travel Insurance:** Consider purchasing travel insurance that covers trip cancellations due to weather-related disruptions.

- **Safety Precautions**: If visiting during hurricane season, ensure you have an evacuation plan and understand local emergency procedures.

Important Contacts and Resources

When traveling through Florida, it's essential to have access to key contacts and resources to ensure a smooth and enjoyable trip. Below are important services and information sources to keep handy.

Emergency Services:

- 911 – For all emergencies, whether medical, fire-related, or law enforcement.

- **Florida Highway Patrol:** For roadside assistance and traffic-related incidents dial *FHP (347) or call 850-617-3416,Option 5.

- **Poison Control:** Call 1-800-222-1222, a 24/7 service for potential poisoning or hazardous exposure.

Visitor Information Centers:

- **Florida Welcome Centers:** Located at major entry points like I-95, I-75, and I-10, these centers provide brochures, maps, and assistance with local attractions. You can find the full list of centers on the Visit Florida website https://www.myflorida.com

- **Tourist Information:** You can call (850) 488-5607 or visit the Visit Florida website www.visitflorida.com for updated travel information, events, and deals.

Medical Assistance:
- **Florida Department of Health:** For health-related resources and updates, visit www.floridahealth.gov

- **Hospitals and Urgent Care :** Major cities like Miami, Orlando, and Tampa have top-tier hospitals (e.g Jackson Memorial Hospital in Miami, Orlando Health in Orlando) and numerous urgent care centers for non-emergency medical attention.

Transportation Services:
- **Florida Department of Transportation:** Visit www.fdot.gov for road conditions, construction updates, and real-time traffic reports.

- **Uber/Lyft:** Both ride-sharing services are widely available across the state, particularly in urban areas.

- **Public Transportation**: Visit local transit websites, such as the Miami-Dade Transit (www.miamidade.gov).

Weather Resources:
- **National Weather Service Florida:** For up-to-date forecasts, storm warnings, and other critical weather updates, visit www.weather.gov/tampa

Wildlife Resources:
- **Florida Fish and Wildlife Conservation Commission (FWC):** For information on wildlife protection and regulations visit www.myfwc.com.

- **Everglades National Park** – For park information, hours, and tours: www.nps.gov/ever

CONCLUSION

Final Tips for a Memorable Trip

As you prepare for your Florida adventure, here are some essential tips to ensure your trip is seamless, enjoyable, and unforgettable:

- **Plan for Weather Variability:** Florida's weather can be unpredictable, with sudden rain showers and hot, humid conditions. Be sure to pack lightweight clothing, sunscreen, and rain gear. It's also wise to check the forecast regularly, especially during the summer when thunderstorms are common.

- **Embrace the Outdoors:** Florida is known for its beautiful outdoor spaces, from its beaches to its national parks. Plan to spend plenty of time outside. Whether you're hiking in the Everglades, kayaking through the Keys, or relaxing on the Gulf Coast beaches, make sure to enjoy the state's diverse landscapes.

- **Rent a Car for Flexibility:** While Florida's cities are well-connected by public transportation, renting a car is highly recommended to fully experience the state. Having your transportation gives you the flexibility to explore hidden gems off the beaten path and take scenic drives like the Historic Tamiami Trail.

- **Book Accommodations in Advance:** Florida is a popular tourist destination, so booking accommodations ahead of time is a smart move, especially during peak seasons like winter and spring break. Whether you're looking for a luxury resort, a cozy beachfront cottage, or a charming boutique hotel, securing your stay early can save you time and stress.

- **Respect Local Wildlife:** Florida is home to diverse wildlife, including manatees, alligators, and numerous bird species. Always respect wildlife by maintaining a safe distance, and avoid feeding or disturbing animals.

- **Explore Beyond the Tourist Spots:** While Florida's famous attractions are a must-see, explore less crowded destinations like charming small towns, local markets, and hidden beaches. These experiences often offer a more authentic taste of Florida's culture.

- **Stay Hydrated and Sun-Safe:** With Florida's intense sun, it's important to stay hydrated and protect yourself from UV rays. Carry a refillable water bottle and apply sunscreen regularly, especially if you plan to spend time outdoors.

Florida Beyond 2025: What's Next

As Florida continues to grow and evolve, the state is poised to offer more exciting opportunities for travelers. From its diverse ecosystems to its vibrant cities, Florida's future is brimming with new experiences, innovations, and attractions.

Sustainability and Eco-Tourism:
As environmental awareness grows, Florida is increasingly focusing on sustainable tourism. The state is developing eco-friendly resorts, enhancing wildlife conservation efforts, and expanding protected natural areas. Expect more eco-tours, green travel options, and eco-lodges that minimize environmental impact while allowing travelers to explore Florida's unique ecosystems responsibly.

New Attractions and Expansions:
Florida's theme parks and resorts are always evolving. New attractions, immersive experiences, and expansions to existing parks promise to keep the state a top destination for thrill-seekers. Future developments in cities like Orlando and Tampa include advanced technology-based experiences, interactive exhibits, and cutting-edge entertainment that push the boundaries of imagination.

Improved Transportation and Accessibility:
Florida is investing in new transportation systems, including high-speed rail networks and expanded public transit options. These improvements will make it easier for travelers to explore the state's diverse regions, from the panhandle to the Keys, enhancing accessibility and convenience.

Cultural and Culinary Growth:
Florida's culinary and cultural scenes are thriving. With a growing emphasis on local food, art, and music, visitors can expect a richer cultural experience, from food festivals celebrating regional dishes to the rise of new art districts in cities like Miami and St. Petersburg.

Florida's future looks bright, with more to discover and explore beyond 2025. The journey is just beginning.

Printed in Dunstable, United Kingdom